WHAT CAN YOU DO?

Bill Gillham

Photographs by Fiona Horne

G.P. Putnam's Sons   New York

What can you do . . .
   with an old car tire?

Give someone a ride!

What can you do...
with all these pillows?

Make a den under the table!

What can you do . . .
   with the bubbles in the bath?

Pretend you have a beard!

What can you do . . .
     with squeezed oranges?

Make monster teeth!

What can you do...
    with a new blue shoe?

Make a bed for your doll!

What can you do . . .
   with a garden hose?

Talk on the telephone!

What can you do . . .
 with these two picture books?

Pull a train through the tunnel!

What can you do...
with empty eggshells?

Make a little boat!

What can you do . . .
  with shiny red cherries?

Make some pretty earrings!

What can you do . . .
    with a pot from the cupboard?

Bang it like a drum!

What can we do . . .
  with bright new towels?

Dress up like kings and queens!

The LOOK AND TALK series combines creative photography with insights from developmental psychology in books that will fascinate young children and stimulate thought and language.

In these books, which are ideal for sharing with adults, children are encouraged to look for differences, search for something hidden, work out where something belongs, and see the possibilities for creative play. They will want to return to the books again and again, to look and talk about what is happening in the vivid action photographs and the lively rhythmic text.

Other LOOK AND TALK books are *Can You See It?*, *What's the Difference?* and *Where Does It Go?*

Dr. Bill Gillham is senior lecturer in the Department of Psychology at Strathclyde University in Scotland.

Fiona Horne was formerly staff photographer in the Audio-visual Department at Strathclyde University and now works as a freelancer.

Text copyright © 1986 Bill Gillham
Photographs copyright © 1986 Bill Gillham and Fiona Horne
First American edition 1986
All rights reserved. This book, or parts thereof, may not be
reproduced in any form without permission in writing from the publishers.
First published by Methuen Children's Books Ltd, London, England.

Library of Congress Cataloging in Publication Data
Gillham, Bill.
  What can you do?

  (A Look and talk book)
  Summary: Photographs and brief text introduce a
variety of objects and experiences and show how they
may be used in play.
  1. Play–Juvenile literature. [1. Play] I. Horne,
Fiona, ill. II. Title. III. Series.
HQ782.G55 1986   155.4'18   85–28137
ISBN 0-399-21324-4
First printing
Printed in Great Britain

SANDUSKY LIBRARY

JAN 1987